CONTENTS

Acknowledgements.........................7

Introduction.............................11

Chapter 1: Let's Do This 15

Chapter 2: The Shit Got Real.................21

Chapter 3: From Shit to Shift.................26

Chapter 4: Do The Work 29

Acknowledgements

For every moment, challenge, experience situation, person, and place that I have walked through and with thus far in my life, My deepest infinite love and gratitude for your part in my journey.

To my angels, guides and council: It takes a village thanks for always having my Back! R&M

We are blessed in life when people amazing people show up and alter your life forever this book is dedicated to a few of them.

To my Mommy, my Seester Kelly, my sunshine Brianna and my hero Joey:
Mahalo, Aloha, Ohana

(you can stop laughing now)

To the first person in my life who Truly showed up, shut up, put up and said yes to every crazy idea and adventure I came up with, including this one. Your love and belief in me has never wavered and because of it, my life is becoming truly unrecognizable. Thank you will never be enough. I love you Fred!

I could literally fill every page of this book with the names of the people whom I love more than words could ever describe. Instead I will again Thank God for filling my life with such abundance and sending me a steady stream of friends, teachers, mentors dolphins, whales, mermaids and beloved earth angels to play, learn and grow with and from.

When the student is ready the teacher will appear and Boy Did They Ever!

Ray Tamayo Thank you for opening the closet door and teaching me the power of I am.

Linda Herrick for removing my issues in my tissues and being an amazing spiritual mentor.

Orsika There really are no Words only a million feels, love and Gratitude for you my soul homie.

Lisa Nichols, Susie Carder and the entire MTM Family & Tribe ~ NAMASTE

Some of my life's greatest lessons have come from my 10 year old nephew Joey. Nonverbal, Autistic they say? However Joeys innate sense of humor and frankness has produced a few perfect words for when something is going on that he is not in alignment with and or not ok with wanna guess what it is? Let's just say if it doesn't feel good, make you happy or fill you with joy.

It's bullshit!

Introduction

Beating yourself up seems to be an easy task for most everyone. It's easy to continually look at your life and see what you want to change and have negative self-talk - telling yourself just how awful you are!

YOU have the ability to stop that starting right now. Today I challenge you. Really look at that person in the mirror. Have the guts, the boldness, and the tenacity to challenge that person. Become aware of the limiting beliefs and mindset that simply block your happiness and joy. I know you have it in you. I know you want it. Now is the time to accept and love yourself right now as you are and be willing to do the work to change the parts of you that you don't like. When you change the you that you think you are, you can change your life.

Throughout this book together, we will use our

tenacity to make the necessary shifts in what you think you believe (the bullshit) and the truth within you. I define tenacity as that light deep within that never gives up. If I were to have quit every time I failed at something, I would not be here today. I feel so blessed in my current life. Not because I've arrived. Not because there isn't anything left to improve. But instead, I have finally reached a place of abundance and possibility. The scarcity mindset I had is behind me. Now, in this moment, I know that the things I see in the mirror are in my control. I can change everything I see. I simply take the next step and show up with gusto and tenacity in this world.

I play full out - every day.

As a "multi-preneur" (running three successful businesses at once), my motivation is to help others find solutions to life's challenges through healing, coaching, inspiration, and encouragement. My businesses help you find happiness, joy, and purpose in your life. Rest assured, however, there was a time, not so long ago, when I felt fed up, depressed, and tired of failing. I was stumbling through my everyday. But my tenacious side would not allow me to quit. So I moved ahead. I pushed through the 140lb weight release, the businesses, the loss, the separation, and the various relationships. All of those blessings wrapped in sandpaper helped shape me into the person here before you. Every ounce of me wanted to make changes in order to be that person who now guides you. Yes, there were days I wanted to quit every minute, but that inner voice kept me moving forward again and again. And again. I know how you feel, how you don't believe this will work for you, how you're too old, fat, dumb, broke - insert your favorite story you tell yourself as to why you aren't worth the life of your dreams.

How many times have you made excuses and told yourself a story about why you can't do, be, have everything you have ever wanted?

What do you say when you talk to yourself?
Let me just say if I can make changes and conquer my limiting beliefs and negative self talk you can and will conquer yours too.

Let's stop believing the bullshit!

Chapter 1: Let's Do This

My story is your story. It's about transforming the limiting beliefs and opportunities that enslave each one of us. Your truest transformation begins with shifting your mind—your thinking patterns. Then, shifting your actions and world views will help strengthen your mind's new residence. By challenging your thoughts, your life will begin transforming.

To better understand limiting beliefs and how they unknowingly affect your life, allow me to share a brief moment of my life with you.

At 10 years old, I attended a birthday party and was picked on for being fat. It wasn't a big deal at the time since kids can be mean, and I was chubby. My aunt tried to reassure me as we sat on the porch. She told me it was going to be okay - she too was picked on and made fun of and lived through it. Soon thereafter, my mother decided to send me to Weight Watchers with my grandmother. My grandmother was always on a diet. At the time, Weight Watchers meetings were in hidden dark basements of churches. It was a creepy place for a young child of 10 years old!

Not only was I afraid, I was humiliated. I had to check in with my little book, wait in line to get on this ginormous scale, and then have someone yell across the room to the note-taker my weight for the week. Are you kidding me? This was the worst form of punishment! But wait, there was more humiliation to be had. All members sat around a circle listening to one another about everyone's struggles and failures with food from the previous week. A not-so-healthy dose of anxiety also encompassed our circles. Applause or looks of pity followed each "sharing moment". If a member lost weight, applause embraced that person. If someone didn't lose weight, small claps and looks of knowing that pain and pity. Ugggh!

Upon finishing up the time of devastation, my Nanny - the wise woman who shared her love, perspective, wisdom and insight to life with me and unknowingly a few of her limiting beliefs as well (I hope you're catching this they come from others too—HELLO) celebrated the week's victories by taking me out for ice cream. Kind gesture, right? It would have been great, had she not announced to what felt like the entire ice cream shop that we were there for Weight Watchers ice cream. As you can imagine, the other kids in line looked at me and smirked. (Nanny meant well. I know this now with my adult mind.) I loved her dearly.

These weekly outings created one hell of story and belief system in this 10 year old girl that unknowingly would continually reinforce for *decades* my feelings of being broken, damaged, different, bad, and that I needed to be fixed. Because without being fixed, (thin) I would not fit in, be accepted, be worthy of anything, and worst of all—I would not be worthy of unconditional love.

It wasn't until I began to do the self-work and went deep to uncover and unpack the feelings and perceptions that created my limiting beliefs, a healthy dose of catholic guilt and really screwed up food relationship practices too.

Does any of this sound familiar?

Can you think of situations or experiences that have caused you to feel and or act a certain way?

We are influenced from a young age and from many sources—familial, religious, cultural, and community. Sadly, some limiting beliefs are passed onto us like family traditions and recipes. My grandmother's potato salad is still second to none!

If you answered with a "Hell ya Tracy! I got piles of 'em!"

TADA - there's the bullshit you believe!

Grab a journal, jot them down ~ awareness is the first step to shifting that shit.

Through countless hours, weeks, months, and years, I have been able to uncover my negative beliefs. This is critical to true healing. All of the negative self-talk throughout the years, hidden deeper and deeper into my subconscious set me up for a life of lack, a life of feeling less than, a life of struggle. All of this became my norm.

You may be wondering how I was able to overcome disappointment and humiliation.

Simple. Through the tenacity of that inner voice. (You have one too, it's your internal GPS) It is that little light inside each of us (Source, God, whatever you call it) that never stops trying, never quits, never gives up. I am grateful to have such a gift from God. Even when the flicker was minimal and it felt like my internal fire was dwindling quietly in the night, it was still present.

Chapter 2: The Shit Got Real

Fifteen years ago, I hit a major depression. My life had run away from me, and I didn't know how to get it back. I experienced unexpected losses and the reality that what I thought was my purpose would not come to be. I kept expecting someone else to fix me - to call me out on my depression, but no one did. This wasn't their fault though. I kept my grief, hurt, and pain buried deep and hidden by a huge mask called my body. I put on the façade of being happy as my weight literally exploded. The weight gain led to health issues. The physical health issues led to mental and emotional health issues. I could no longer perform simple tasks such as laundry and fetching the mail. After such simple activities, I needed to sit and rest. Literally.

One day, I was done. I was done with all of it. So, I took action. The flame grew a little brighter. I went to the doctor to get some blood work done. I was so anemic at the time, that I needed an iron transfusion. I was barely showing up in the world at this point. I truly believe that the disease in my mind was causing the disease in the body.

My depression held me captive in my bed. I felt my life was without purpose. I remember doing minimal housework as quickly as I could before my husband came home so that he thought I had actually done something that day. I was doing it. I was successfully living a life without purpose and had a pile of limiting beliefs.

One night, I was startled awake by a voice telling me to "Get up, get up now"! So I sat up and looked around the room. I was alone. But the voice, that voice I heard was distinct and clear. I got out of bed and started pacing the kitchen, my heart pounding with every breath I took. I knew I had to move my body. Nothing else mattered at that particular moment. This my friends, is what you call a wake-up call.

From that moment on, I took the one remaining part of me and moved. I took that tenacity, embraced it, and moved forward. No more being stagnant. No more lying around the house. Each day, I forced myself to get up, get dressed, eat healthier, go to the doctor, and get honest with myself. It meant I was going to have to change everything.

At one point, I was told, "Examine the worst parts of yourself." (Thanks Ray!) At the time, all I could think about were the negative parts of me. The parts I hated, the parts I hid from everyone. I began thinking about that, looking at my belief systems. What was keeping me stuck in that negative space - to be willing to live a life with no purpose and no desire? I was now medically super obese. My thought was,

"No one is going to take me seriously with any businesses that I create until I get myself together and release this weight." It is important to realize this was yet another limiting belief.

My husband loved me. He supported me. That was great. What wasn't great was that I didn't know how to accept, love or support myself. My negative beliefs allowed my tenacious nature to fade away. So, I was stuck in this negatively empowering frame of mind. Yuck! Learning to create momentum was difficult, but I had to do it. Personal development and digging deep to heal played a major role in this movement. I had to get real with myself. I had to ask the tough questions: Why do I feel this way? Where do my beliefs come from? Are these beliefs real and true? Oh man, were these questions difficult?! Difficult, yes. But necessary.

Momentum, awareness, and willingness to question everything got me far enough out of the depression. I constantly asked myself why I haven't yet achieved my goals. It became more and more important that I dig deeper and deeper in order to bring myself higher and higher. Through the course of several years, I have learned how to examine things from the past that created the negative limiting beliefs and create new beliefs that keep me from limiting myself. (The work's never done BTW; it's like pulling weeds in the garden) These new beliefs, though, have changed my life. I was finally able to shift the shit I thought I believed and crawl out of that place that kept me sad, unhappy, and without passion.

Chapter 3: From Shit to Shift

I work and work to continually grow my spirit and mind every day. If you decided to read this book due to life, weight, and or self-image challenges, I know exactly how you feel. It does not matter if your struggle is on one end of the spectrum or the other.

The struggle, the challenge, the need to get out of that prison, is the same. The steps are the same. The motivation is the same. Until you begin focusing on your limiting beliefs, and changing those, the outcome will always be the same.

I took the momentum and frankly, fear that came from that scary night - a night that could have even been my last night if I hadn't gotten up - that momentum got me far enough to focus on myself just a little bit more. And that's what I encourage you to do. Let's not look outside ourselves for the solution. There is no quick fix. I can tell you even today, at my current weight, there are goals and scale markers I will achieve; though I am simply not there yet. I can however, see myself getting up tomorrow, grateful for my abundant life, making good choices, eating healthy, live foods, and exercising. I will continue loving my life and loving myself. Most importantly, I will positively adjust my actions, my attitude and the way I treat myself every day.

Maybe you're there too. Maybe you're like me - you grew up with messages that that made you feel unworthy or created a lack mentality.

What are the stories you believe about yourself? I look back now at what I truly believed most of my life. I believed that my weight made me broken. I wasn't like others and therefore needed to be "fixed." One of the biggest limiting beliefs that we latch onto is that we won't be better *until*... whatever comes after that for you. That's the belief you need to get past, because you're already perfect just as you are. There may be some other challenges that you take on in your life - to tenaciously choose to change - but that's not going to make you better afterwards. You're amazing right now.

Chapter 4: Do The Work

How did I move out of my depression? I started challenging my limiting beliefs every day. I learned to question why I was feeling a certain way and then reach for a better feeling following the Emotional Guidance Scale. (Google it) I had to get to that place where I told myself that I will do whatever it takes to live a full and wonderful life. I found affirmations. I began to question the reasons behind why I felt unworthy. I needed to dig deep and tell myself I was worthy now.

Not "someday". Not "I'll be worthy when…" Not "I'll be loved if…" I kept asking myself, "Tracy, why are you worthy now?"

In your present self, you are more than likely going to have to challenge everything that comes up for you. And I mean *everything*! Give up living in the center of all of those misguided beliefs. Question everything that comes up. Give yourself grace, time and forgiveness. Give yourself permission to no longer accept those limiting beliefs. Look at them through different lenses. Continue to consciously look at the positive in order to shed the old thought patterns. Find that tenacious part of you that won't allow you to give up and give in. I know it's there. If it's lost deep, deep, deep inside, don't worry. I'm here to stand with you right now, in this moment and the next and the next, because I know you are worthy. You have something to give. I challenge you to be tenacious and shift the shit!

It's easy to look in the mirror and see that body part that you're not happy with, here is my challenge for you. Pick a part of your body that you do like. Maybe you're not happy with your flabby arms, but you have a very pretty smile. Maybe you wish your nose was different, but you have beautiful eyes. Begin talking to yourself about how beautiful your smile and eyes are rather than telling yourself about the blemish that you see. Continue to go back and challenge your limiting beliefs until you will eventually begin to find that that particular limiting belief just isn't as strong. Eventually, as you go back and look at that "flaw", it's just gone. You don't see it anymore - you see your own beauty.

There have been times in my life when I did okay. When I thought that I was good enough. And yet there will always be people that are more than willing to point out all the ways that you are not enough. DO NOT LISTEN TO THEM! Replace their negative beliefs with your own positive truths. Replace the negativity with positive affirmations about who you truly are. When those old belief systems pop up, when people say things and make negative comments to you, call it what it is,

Bullshit!   Knock them back. Don't accept them.

It's a mental connection that will allow us to deal with the deeper issues. Practicing self-love so we can go to our positive belief systems to anchor what we have learned and practiced. In turn, we develop a better self-worth. Without the healthy, mental connection, no amount of self-suffering is going to be permanent. You can diet for your entire life - or binge and purge - or whatever your Achilles' heel may be - and get nowhere. Being healthy in your mind is the only way to true healing in your body.

I can attest to the above actions, because I've been there. I've tried every diet. I've made myself suffer through countless, wasted hours at various programs. I failed over and over and over again. Why? Because I did not realize my own self-worth. My mind absolutely had to get to the place where I felt worthy of life. When I finally accepted myself and decided to take care of myself, the weight with which I had struggled my entire life - shed.

Being vulnerable and loving you through all your challenges, I am here to be by your side, to let you know: You are good enough! & You are worthy of love! Other people's opinions about you just don't matter. Now is the time for you to realize that you can love yourself. What you feel about YOU is what's absolute and most important.

If I could go back in time, to my ten-year-old me, I would tell her she is unconditionally loved for who she is exactly as she is and she's special. Maybe hearing those words would have eliminated countless years of struggles and suffering. What would you tell your hurt inner child?

You've spent entirely too much time putting other people's opinions and thoughts ahead of your own. These opinions and thoughts have created a lack of self-worth. In turn, other people's negativity and limiting beliefs have become your own. But they don't need to be. You can change all of it - if you're willing. I know you are able.

Now is the time to let those beliefs go. Stop accepting that you won't be anything and know that you are already amazing. It is time for you to ignite that fire within. It is time for you rise up and blaze in to the best version of you. It is time to ignore other people's standards for your life.

Take a deep breath! As difficult as it may feel inside, as you read these challenging words, I want you to know that your life is just starting. Your worth has nothing to do with how you look, where you live or how much you make.

It has nothing to do with what you've been through in the past, or what other people say to or about you. You are worth it! You can love yourself. As you learn this, you can be of service to others. First you must love yourself before being able to pour into others. As the saying goes, "You can't fill other's cups if yours is empty." Don't allow others beliefs to deter you from living your authentic self.

In order to make this all practical, I have a few recommendations for you. Today is the day you can begin shifting your limiting beliefs.

First, get two pieces of paper. On the first sheet, list all the negative things that you have ever said about yourself. On the other sheet, list all the things that are true and positive about yourself. You don't have to believe these things just yet.

Go back to the first sheet - with the negative

things. Beside each negative belief, write something that can challenge the thought. For example, you see a flaw on your face in the mirror. Immediately shift your attention to the positive. (i.e. My nose is HUGE. My ears are adorable!) Do this for every item on your list. For each one of the negative things you say about yourself, give yourself something new, happy, and positive that you can say about yourself.

Now let's take the list of all the things that you don't believe yet. The first question to ask yourself is, "Why?" Why don't you believe that about yourself? Some of the beliefs are just too big. We don't have enough experience to see them clearly. This is a little step in that right direction to help you to believe it now. Next to each of beliefs, write down something that you can believe right now. Begin to replace your limiting beliefs; both the negative things you say about yourself and those positive things you believe about yourself.

Second, there are so many great affirmations available to you. Find the affirmations that speak loudest to your spirit. Write them on index cards or put them on sticky notes all around your house & car. Yes. Seriously. Remember to use all of the rooms in your home. Your laundry space. Your bathroom. Your closet. Your pantry or cupboards. Your refrigerator—inside your refrigerator and freezer. EVERYWHERE!!! Surround yourself with positive affirmations about how you can do it and how amazing you are! You want to be inundated with the positive affirmations. You want to be able to move through your home and find a positive affirmation in every nook, cranny, and corner. You need to see and say your affirmations continually in order to start feeling each affirmation as your new reality. (channeling Mel Robbins here... "There's neuroscience behind writing them out and even more saying them out loud too.") 5,4,3,2,1 Let's do this daily.

Third, begin journaling your journey. If you have been journaling, then take it a step deeper. Write down all of your emotions. What feeling(s) makes you want to reach for your favorite escape? (food, wine, etc?) What sabotages your goals? What event(s) happened to make you speak so negatively about yourself? As you begin to explore the root of your emotions, you can then begin to also challenge them and learn new ways, better ways, to be able to handle the situations that come into your life.

Lastly, meditation and visualization. I believe both are imperative. Every day I spend quiet time listening to a mediation or some of my favorite music - taking time to stop my brain and simply be still. What you think about is what you bring about. However, feeling is the secret. You need to visualize - visualize yourself at that next step.

You don't have to visualize yourself at the destination. But, can you visualize yourself taking the next step and physically feeling into it as being accomplished? Say something positive about yourself today. Will you try feeling happy, smiling, or allowing somebody that loves you to tell you that they love you—really take it in and receive it?

You see, when those things happen in your life, and they will, until you're open to them, you won't see them. In order to be able to see them, you have to first visualize them. Set your mind's eye on seeing how good it feels to do, be, have all that you desire. Ask and it is given. Wait in expectancy and see how exciting it is as the universe brings that about!

I know that life has been tough. I also know that life is going to get better. I hope that from here on out you hear my voice in your ear forever. You hear me telling you that you are so special. You are strong. You are worthy. You have a gift to share with the world.

Love yourself enough to know that you're helping others simply by embracing and being your authentic self.

I know without a shadow of a doubt, that deep within you, you are tenacious.

You are powerful.

You are Amazing.

And You Don't Believe Bullshit.

You're Awesome and I love you!

To Contact Tracy or be notified
of upcoming events to be
further inspired to grow,
Please join her at
www.inspiringu2grow.com
or @tracyinspires on Instagram
or Facebook

Cover Credits To:

Amy Bissonnette Photography Chicago,IL

Orsika Julia @ Believe, Inspire, Heal, LLC

Hey Cookie! Remember....

It's all Bullshit! xoxo

42